The Life Story of Pigeon

Moving from trees to windows, a
side-effect of deforestation

As seen by Marsha White

Once upon a time, there was a

pigeon that made its nest in

the corner of a big window,

the window was half-open and

sheltered the pigeon enough

to rest its twigs and dry grass.

The pigeon used to get straws,

wood, feathers and branches every day. Often it used to rest in the other corner of the window when another pigeon used to help get the remaining stuff for building the nest. Both of them built a small nest in a few days' time.

The two pigeons then vanished

for some time.

After few days, two small eggs

appeared in the nest. The two

pigeons would sit on the white eggs for hours continuously daily. When one would go to get the food the other would rest itself on the eggs with care. The window seemed to be a bit tight and the mother pigeon pushed it a little further with her nose to conveniently juxtapose between the gaps. The father pigeon came in for a while and rested himself on the eggs when the mother went for a small flight in the open sky.

The pigeons never seemed to rest except for building the nest, searching for food and resting on the eggs. That was the daily routine. One day another pigeon flew into the window and the mother pigeon became restless, it

signalled to the other to go

away but it did not go. The

father pigeon then came and

fought wing-to-wing for few

minutes after which the new

pigeon flew away. The father

pigeon guarded the window

while the mother looked after

the eggs.

Two weeks passed. The egg

hatched and a small chick

appeared. It was light orange

in colour and was looking big

enough to sit in that egg for so

many days. The mother fed the

baby pigeon with some food

by opening its beak. The baby bird took its food from the mother's mouth. There were soft chirps from the baby bird. Its head had small feathers like uncombed hair and it was not able to move except for its beak that turned in all directions along with its head while chirping.

The other egg also hatched

after two days and another

birdie appeared in the nest.

The father would sit on the

other side of the open window

some times and on the other corner at other times. The mother pigeon never left the babies alone except for once or twice a day to get more grass to make the nest warm for the two in the cold nights.

The two pigeons took good

care of the new tiny pigeons.

The two little ones would chirp

endlessly during the day and

night and they would get food

from the old one's beak. The

mother would climb onto the

two tiny ones to make them

warm and would sit in the

same way that she sat on the

eggs. Sometimes they would

sleep but at other times they

would push and punch their

mother with the soft heads and

the mother would move to

give them space to stare into

the open space. At other

times, the two siblings would

relentlessly fight with each

other poking their soft beaks

onto each other's bodies.

After two weeks, small wings

appeared and the beaks

seemed to become stronger

and bigger. The older sibling

would try to lift its body off the

window slab while opening its

wings that seemed to be

bigger than itself. The younger sibling would simply stare at the talent shown by the other. The mother pigeon would watch from the corner of the other window. There was a small burp every time the bird tried to fly, indicating that it was making a conscious effort to spread its wings and fly to search for its mother, or was it a

frustration at the inability to fly?

Soon the mother pigeon came

and sat upon the two siblings

again; the two were much

bigger and were strong

enough to push away the big

pigeon. The pigeon gave some

way by moving a bit away

from the chicks. The two would

then sit cosily against one another and poke their beaks onto one another's bodies. The father pigeon would come and feed the babies with his beak. The baby pigeons seemed to enjoy with both their parents on either side and they made busy chirps as if it was party time.

Days passed and the two

pigeons looked bluer than

earlier. The bodies turned from

orange to light blue to navy

blue with spots on the wings

and now they seemed to

20

belong to the family of

pigeons. They also seemed

bulkier and did not stop

punching their parents with the

beaks.

Meanwhile the other pigeons

took to their chores and there

was another pair of tiny

pigeons in another window,

the residence sheltered more

than 20 pigeons in different

houses. They all searched for

food and water and whenever

food was thrown into any

window, there was a heavy

scuttle amongst the pigeons

with some hovering away the

others while poking into the

food lying on the walls.

The pigeons seemed to enjoy

the fight. They fought and got

the food for their little ones.

Each pigeon family occupied

a window on each house. They

would make noise throughout

the day and rest in silence

during the nights. The little ones

would chirp even during the

nights.

The pigeons would stroll on the

windows. They would pick the

leftovers on the windows, peep

into the houses through the

netted windows and would

push against the mesh to enter

into the rooms while fighting

with other pigeons.

One pigeon was a loner and would sit on the windows with one of its feet folded inside. It would stand on one leg on the window for hours without making any noise. The other leg was fine but the pigeon was more interested in not

using it. Was it a sage among

the pigeons? Was it

meditating?

The pigeons would become

attention of small kids, crying

babies and old grandmothers

soothing their infants. A maid

would get the crying baby and

show the resting baby pigeons and tell how the pigeons have built nests in the windows. The baby would stop crying for a moment but would resume as soon as he understood that he could not lay his hands on the birds on the distant window.

Day by day, the baby pigeons

looked older and bigger.

Sometimes they looked same

as any other pigeon. But they

could not fly. Still, the wings

were large enough to be

flapped against the window

whenever the pigeon tried to

lift itself up by fluttering. The size

was so similar to that of grown-

ups that the young pigeons

had to vacate their usual

cuddling spots in the nook of

the window sill. They occupied

the open end of window to

allow themselves more space for movement and fluttering. The only way to distinguish their age was by the soft hair on the top of their heads, which was not present on the mature birds.

One day, a non-family pigeon

came from the other side and

started poking into the new

growing ones. The new ones

could not fly, so the mother

pigeon came to their rescue

when she cuddled the two

siblings in the nook and sat

guarding between them and

the rogue pigeon that poked

into the mother for some time

and flew away after hearing

noises from inside the house.

The mother did not give up the

guard until the father pigeon also came. Then the big babies started picking onto some food lying on the window sill. The house owner made sure of scattering some bird food that he got especially from the market for the pigeons. His wife also would scatter some food on the other kitchen window so that the fighting rogue pigeons and others would not disturb the growing ones for food. The family of the four pigeons rested on the window by one of the bedrooms. Though the babies looked more robust, they could not gather enough strength to lift their bodies into thin air until after few weeks.

The soft meek shrill chirps and baby hair made them look young. It was only after over two months into their birth that the pigeons could fly after turning into full-fledged mature ones. Small baby pigeons and old baby pigeons are thus equally vulnerable. Only the mature ones can fly. At times, it seemed to the owner's daughter that danger was imminent, given that the window was located on the house on fourth floor of the building and that cats prowled on the grounds. The owner's wife announced that they would not allow any more pigeon nests after the existing ones would learn to fly. The

reasons were multi-fold. The

window became dirty with

pigeon droppings, straws,

leaves, twigs that in turn gave

rise to mosquitoes at home. The

birds tried to break open the

net and enter into the room

through the window whenever

they fought or felt colder. Also,

it was a new responsibility to

guard and feed the new birds.

They would continue to feed

the birds by throwing food on

the windows.

The pigeons seemed to have

their own dreams. The tiny ones

held the dream of flying like

their mother. The old ones had

their dreams of defeating

others while snatching away the food. Still others had the dreams of protecting their young ones and seeing them grow. Some had the dreams of going over the windows again and again in search of an entrance into the houses themselves. Some dreams lived and some perished. We are

cutting the trees and taking up

deforestation. The side-effect is

that pigeons are giving up

trees and moving nests to

houses and windows.

A lesson!

The trees and forests should not be mercifully laid to rest. This is the clearest lesson emerging out of the pigeons for us.

As the young ones grew, the parent pigeons wonderfully cleaned the window sill, spic & span, by scratching upon the droppings, and stale nest material. The mother pigeon brought fresh green twigs into the window giving it a beautiful green look, better than any interior designer's work. Before

anybody could guess, what

the pigeon wanted to do the

pigeon's sense of responsibility

was clear. Though the little

ones grew bigger, they still

could not fly. They could

merely walk across the space

over window sill. The parent

pigeons were sensible enough

not to let their birdies dwell in dirt. The fresh green branches and twigs were carefully picked by the mother pigeon in setting up her new nest!

Soon after the young ones grew and flew away, the mother pigeon laid two more eggs. The mother now shifted her attention to the eggs. The younger of the two came in

and sat during the nights as the

mother sat upon the eggs. The

older one came in less

frequently. Gradually, the

pigeon siblings stopped sitting

in the window except for

feeding on the grain in other

windows too.

The house-owners were impressed by pigeons' dedication and did not do anything but were tempted to allow the well-disciplined pigeon continue extend its family.

After all, it's the same world for all of us.

About the author-

Marsha has been constantly

observing pigeons for more

than a year before penning

the brief biography on pigeons.

Marsha has written several books for kids, including the series in Ria's Life – Ria's Holiday, The Big Book Mission, and The Softer Side & The Marriage.